*The Regular Effect:
How To Release Yourself
From The Comfort Of Being Normal*

by Shiv Rad

© Copyright 2018 Shiv Rad

ISBN 978-1-63393-605-8

All rights reserved. No part of this publication may be reproduced, stored in a retrieval system, or transmitted in any form or by any means—electronic, mechanical, photocopy, recording, or any other—except for brief quotations in printed reviews, without the prior written permission of the author.

Published by

THE REGULAR EFFECT

HOW TO RELEASE YOURSELF
FROM THE COMFORT OF BEING

NORMAL

SHIV
RAD

www.ShivRad.com

This book is dedicated to my parents, whom I love very much. To my sisters, Vana and Sharda, thanks for having my back. To my brother-in-law, Dr. Ravi Asi, thanks for being a true brother, and to my niece, Anaiya, who has just joined our family, welcome, princess.

TABLE OF CONTENTS

	FOREWORD	1
	PREFACE	3
1.	THE REGULAR GUY	5
2.	BECOMING THE TRUE "YOU"	11
3.	SET YOURSELF FREE	18
4.	THE DEATH OF A MENTOR	24
5.	THE IMPORTANCE OF BRANDING	32
6.	SHOP 'TILL YOU DROP—THE POWER OF NETWORKING	40
7.	EXCUSES, EXCUSES, EXCUSES	46
8.	THE BEST MEDICINE IN THE CABINET: LAUGHTER	56
9.	PROTECTING YOUR ENTHUSIASM	64
10.	EVEN ALI HAD A MENTOR	69
11.	FEAR OF THE UNKNOWN	76
12.	OPTIMIZING YOUR WEALTH	84
13.	TURNING A NEGATIVE INTO A POSITIVE—THE FULL CIRCLE	90
14.	BREAK FREE	96

FOREWORD

I'VE KNOWN SHIV all his life. We grew up together in Toronto. I've been so proud to see the man he's become, and I am honored to introduce *The Regular Effect*.

Let me begin by saying I'm a big believer in the concept of being "irregular." I left a career as a computer programmer and ended up going to medical school in my thirties after I was married with kids. Taking the road less travelled was daunting, but has been a wonderfully enriching and transformative experience. Embracing the unknown and stepping out of your comfort zone is something I can't recommend highly enough.

Shiv, however, has turned this into something of an art. Making a deliberate, daily effort to conquer fear, doubt, and insecurity is his passion. He refuses to let societal expectations, social pressure, or self-imposed limitations hinder the pursuit of his goals.

When he set his sights on losing weight, the family watched in amazement as he transformed his body through relentless discipline and dedication. A few years later, when he decided to move from Canada to Australia, he dispelled all our concerns by flourishing in his new surroundings.

What is truly admirable, though, is his passion for helping others realize this same potential in themselves. I've become an avid listener of the Shiv Show podcast and the stories of persistence and triumph he shares there are inspiring.

Shiv is the real deal. A tireless worker, fierce advocate, and sincere family man. When he comes home, he makes time for everyone. He gives selflessly and is so humble that you'd never guess he is as successful as he has become. He's just as comfortable addressing a crowd of hundreds as playing trucks with my sons.

Although he is half a world away, his love and care make him seem nearby. I've seen him grow from a boy to a man; I knew him before and after his weight loss, and I watched him grieve his father. Watching him reinvent himself has been nothing short of extraordinary. Shiv inspires me, challenges me, and even though I'm the older cousin, he drives me to be better. For that, I'll always be grateful to him.

In these pages, you'll find his mission statement for life. Honest, unapologetic, and raw, just like the man. So read on and be stimulated, provoked, and motivated. Be encouraged to make a change for the better—to step out and find that part inside that yearns to be a little less "regular."

—ANDREW RAMADEEN, MD PHD

PREFACE

THE REGULAR EFFECT, as defined by yours truly, is society's perception of normality, drilled into our minds from a young age. The "norm" is for everyone to have the same goals, act a certain way, and follow the same rules. To be regular means to be the same. This book is about breaking away from the *regular effect*, and finding ways to be irregular in your society—mixed, of course, with my own personal stories and experiences. Changing your atmosphere, surrounding yourself with different people, and doing things differently are just a few ways to break the *regular effect*. When I was writing this book, I had one goal in mind: to help *one* person break out of their comfort zone and crack the *regular effect*. The *regular effect* surrounds us all, and we don't even notice the power it has. Break away, and I guarantee you peace of mind.

I've written this book to help people unleash their true self. I really don't want this book to be one that you skim and put back on the shelf. *The Regular Effect* is meant to be a book that you keep referring to, so you'll notice a blank page after every chapter, with some space to jot down what you've learned and what your next steps will be. I've done this with a few of the books I've read, and it has been a huge help. Of course, notes are not mandatory, but they have helped me when referring back. Along with the space for notes, I've added a few quotes after every chapter that are tailored to the specific chapter. I've narrowed it down to the top quotes that keep me motivated on the chapter's specific topic.

Helping people is what it's all about—I truly believe that my experiences, when put on paper, can help people who are going through similar experiences. If you aren't going through the same experiences, that's okay! I'm still here to help you break away from the norm. Changing the way you move, the way you speak, and the way you work is all part of the game. To be honest with you, I will tell you right here and now that a majority of the people you surround yourself with won't like that you're changing. I had heaps of people telling me that I had changed, but my answer to them all was "Damn right."

This simply means that you're doing something right, so I hope you embrace the change you're about to experience!

CHAPTER 1

THE REGULAR GUY

"They laugh at me because I'm different;
I laugh at them because they're all the same."
—UNKNOWN

AS I SIT in my room in Sydney, Australia, I look around and I see a few things. I see a stack of books on my desk, some Toronto paraphernalia on the wall, a large picture of my father, and a bottle opener I bought in Trinidad a few years ago. It's funny how a few simple items can explain who you are, no matter how small or large they are. The books represent my willingness to learn and expand my mind. The Toronto gear represents the love I have for my hometown and the people in it. The picture of my dad, which is dearest to me, represents security and a higher being. Lastly, the bottle opener probably sums up my love of a few occasional beers after a stressful day at work. We've all heard the saying "You are the average of the five people you associate with most." Well, folks, I'm a strong believer that your physical surroundings also show who you are.

"The regular guy" is who I thought I was. As a matter of fact, I strived to be the regular guy. Growing up, my parents told me to work hard, find a good job, get a good education ("because no one can ever take that away from you"—I'm sure every West Indian child has heard this many times!), and then you will land a good job. After landing a good job, you can get married, have kids, and live with your parents until they pass on. Sound fun? I don't think so.

That is the regular guy mentality that I grew up hearing every day. Do I blame my parents? Absolutely not. When they were growing up, I'm certain they heard the same thing from their parents. Back in the day, things were different. But now, we live in the twenty-first century, and it's up to us to build our future.

Our generation is completely different, with no excuses. This time around, we're not being told to work the regular nine-to-five jobs, or become a doctor, lawyer, or engineer in order to succeed. Society has completely turned it around and is now telling us to rip away from the typical ways of working.

Do I agree? Absolutely! Don't get me wrong—I have a nine-to-five job, which I love, but the benefits of breaking away from the norm can be exponential if done the right way. Absolutely nothing is wrong with working eight to ten hours a day for a company of your choice. If this is your passion, I strongly urge you to do it and succeed. But ask yourself how you're using your time outside of the job. Are you productive when you get home from work? Or do you turn on the TV until you fall asleep?

The *regular effect* really means that you are surrounded by regular people doing regular things, and the fact that everything is so regular means that you yourself become regular. Did I use the word *regular* enough to explain that? I think so. It's important to drill the word into your brain so that you have the ability to change. Why not become *irregular*? Why not do things differently from what your parents, or friends, your school, and even your boss have taught you? There is nothing wrong with doing the irregular thing once in a while. By not doing what everyone else is doing, you're already stepping out of your comfort zone.

The comfort zone is a very dark place for me, as I'm sure it is for millions of people. First, ask yourself what a comfort zone means. Is it a place you feel secure, safe, and protected so that you don't have to step outside and feel vulnerable?

Here is what the *Oxford English Dictionary* tells us about the comfort zone: "A settled method of working that requires little effort and yields only barely acceptable results." That is bang on! The comfort zone is one of the worst places to be in. Do you think your coworker was just promoted to director of sales because they stayed in their comfort zone?

Do you think Barack Obama stayed in his safe little corner when he was running for president? Do you think that when someone makes a decision to lose weight and get healthy and fit, they stay in their comfort zone? Hell no!

If you want to achieve the next, best thing, whether it is in your career, your lifestyle, your relationship, or any other situation, you need to step out of that safe and secure mindset.

Every morning, I wake up and I say two mottoes to myself: "Be who you say you are," and "I am uncomfortable being comfortable."

The second motto means so much to me. Imagine what we could accomplish if we stepped out of our little zone for a few minutes every day. I'm not asking you to always put yourself in awkward situations if you're not used to them—that will take time and practice. I am asking you to risk discomfort, even if it's for ten minutes a day. The next time you have a meeting at work, put your hand up and ask a question. The next time you're at a gym, ask someone for advice, or give someone advice. The next time you're in an elevator with an awkward silence (we all love that, am I right?), say hello to the person across from you. I can guarantee that if you step out of your zone for ten minutes for thirty days, it will no longer seem like a chore. It will become your lifestyle, which you've just changed by simply changing the way you normally do something.

Being different can give you so much power. It can differentiate you from others at work, it can differentiate you at a bar when you're trying to pull a few numbers, and it can differentiate your mindset. I consider myself very different from a lot of people I surround myself with, and I am 110 percent okay with that. The fact is that I like being different, and I like to surround myself with different personalities.

For example, my flat-mate is a very patient person, and that's a trait I admire. I spend a lot of time with him, learning what goes through his mind as he makes decisions. Unlike me, he thoroughly thinks through the implications and rewards, whereas I sometimes act way too quickly and mess everything up! It's always good to be different, and to hang around with people who possess different skills to you. Time is something we can never get back, so you'd better make sure the people you spend your time with are worth it. Remember, proximity is power!

NOTES

"To be normal is the ideal of the unsuccessful."
—CARL JUNG

CHAPTER 2

BECOMING THE TRUE "YOU"

"The whole point of being alive is to evolve into the complete person you were intended to be."
—OPRAH WINFREY

AS A YOUNG child, I struggled to define who I was, who I wanted to be, and what I wanted to be when I grew up. I went from doctor to astronaut to lawyer to engineer to teacher, and somehow, I landed in sales, and am now an author and podcaster, among many other titles! Things change with time, and that is perfectly okay. Some of you may be struggling to figure out who you are, and this will be a constant question until the very end. *Who am I?* cannot be answered simply. As time goes on, as you have different experiences, as people come and go, and as you move to different places, things will change, and most importantly, *you* will change.

If you asked me who I was five years ago, my answer would be completely different from what it is now. Five years ago, I was just entering my career as a salesman at a tech company. I was living in Brampton, Ontario with my parents and sisters, and I had no ambition to do anything else. I was content. I was in my comfort zone.

As time went by and I experienced different life events, I changed. Fast forward five years, I am now living in Sydney, Australia—somewhere I *never* thought I would be, or even visit. I am still a salesman, but now at a different tech company. Am I the same person? Some would argue that I am, but I am telling you that I am completely different. The only thing that remains the same is that I work for a tech company. Other than that, my mind has changed, my body changed, and my mission changed. I have come to realize that opportunities are endless, and the world is a small place.

Friends and family members often ask me why I moved across the globe, and why I left everyone I know, and how I'm surviving without anyone in Australia with me. My answer to them is very simple, and it all ties back to wanting to break out of the *regular effect*. The move across the globe involved a plane ticket, two suitcases, a backpack, and some minor planning.

A transfer opportunity with my job in Toronto made things a bit easier. I would recommend that anyone moving across the world have a job lined up. This helped with the situation, but in reality, it was just a plane ride (or two) away. When I moved, I knew of two friends from university living in Sydney, and that was it. I didn't move in with them—I wanted to do everything myself, and challenge myself. I wanted to find my own place to live, meet new people, and have exciting, new experiences.

My move to Australia has definitely changed who I am. It has cured me of the *regular effect* syndrome, and I've realized that the world is a lot smaller than we think. We are taught from a young age that everything is so far away. In my experience, we are also taught that leaving your family and friends is wrong.

But if you really sit and think about it, you'll realize that your family and friends (mainly family) simply fear letting you go. Although my parents were immigrants to Canada from Guyana and Trinidad, I was taught that I needed to stick with my family and never leave until I was married. Marriage was the key—it was always the big thing.

Now that I have moved to Australia, do I think I left my family? Not one bit. Does my family think I deserted them? Absolutely not. I guarantee that if you ask your friends or family if they would move across the world, the majority will say, "I can't." We grow up with society telling us that we can't do things—that we need some sort of acceptance to do what we want to do. That is the *regular effect* and, ladies and gentlemen, *the force is strong* (there had to be at least one *Star Wars* reference in this book!).

Today I am the Shiv who is in sales, living in Australia. I am a huge family guy and a good friend. I hope to God that the majority of my family and friends will agree with that! I am a risk-taker and a guy who likes to help others. These things won't change, because I strongly believe that you are selling your brand every single day. If you ask me who I am five years from now, I can guarantee that I will have tweaked my statement and added even more attributes.

Life is about growing, it's about learning, and it's about adding to the personality that you possess and the brand that you portray and sell. Within the next five years, I'll definitely be making a few more "mistakes" along my journey. I, for one, am looking forward to them. Mistakes teach us and define us. You win or you learn—the only way to perfect something is by making a few mistakes first!

How do I constantly work on my personality? What I do, and what I encourage everyone to do, is constantly challenge themselves. I speak up whenever I get a chance—for example, if I have a point to make or a question to ask. Although that action may seem simple, it gets me out of my comfort zone and into the game. I try to learn something new every single day, whether it's through a little bit of reading, going to a seminar, or watching a few how-to videos on YouTube. Everything helps, and it also gives you things to talk about when meeting people with different interests . . . and trust me, the how-to videos help on awkward dates when you run out of things to talk about!

Here are just a few quick tips on how to define the *true you*:

Think of the type of person you want to be tomorrow, in five years, ten years, fifteen years, twenty years.

Now *write it down.*

Post this in your room, your bathroom, above your kitchen sink, on your desk at work.

Ask the people who know you well what they think your current personality traits are.

Finally, summarize who you want to be in one sentence, starting with: "I strive to be someone who is . . ."

I call this a *true you* statement. My current *true you* statement reads: *I strive to be someone who is respectful, family-oriented, and always willing to lend a helping hand.*

Another question I like to throw at my family and friends is "What makes you happy?" Often the answer is money, power, alcohol, food (sign me up!), happiness, the safety of their children, and the list goes on. The real question is *Where does your happiness stem from?*

If you would like to know what makes me happy, here it is—I feel happiest when I help someone. Simple as that. Happiness is meant to be simple. It shouldn't be something you need to dig twenty feet underground for. Simplify what makes you happy so that you can always find a way to laugh and smile during the tough times. I love helping people move houses (though not at 5 a.m. every Saturday, friends)! I love helping people through tough times, I love helping people build their Ikea furniture, and the absolute best feeling comes from helping people regain their confidence. No matter who I meet, I will always find something to like, and I will tell them. Yes, I've been called a *flirt* by a woman or two, but when I compliment someone and make them smile or make them genuinely happy, I am at my highest point of happiness. See that? I keep it extremely simple! So, if you ever get a chance to meet me, know that you have a genuine compliment coming your way.

How do you find out who you truly are? I can't give you a generic answer that will work for every individual, but I can tell you how I found out who I was.

First, let's think of the *regular effect* and what it does to society as a whole. The *regular effect* tells people who they should be, the way they should act, and what is accepted by society. The first step in becoming the *true you* is to recognize the *regular effect*. All my life, society told me to do things a certain way, but I decided that it was time to actually question it. After realizing there was an issue, I started to think of my future and who I wanted to be in my adulthood. I definitely didn't want to remain the shy, timid guy—I wanted to become the best version of myself.

The way I found my true self was in realizing my potential, and actually telling myself that I could do something, instead of listening to society tell me that I couldn't.

NOTES

"Life isn't about finding yourself,
it's about creating yourself."
—UNKNOWN

How do you define happiness?

_____
_____
_____
_____
_____
_____
_____
_____
_____
_____
_____
_____
_____
_____
_____
_____
_____

CHAPTER 3

SET YOURSELF FREE

"Shut out the physical world. Control the mind.
Then you will become free."
—*BHAGAVAD GITA*

IF YOU GREW up the way I did, you would've noticed multiple constraints. Before I get into them, I will say this: I didn't realize they were constraints until I grew up. When I talk about social constraints to my friends and family, it becomes even clearer how much those limits control peoples' lives. These constraints include: societal control of freedom, respect for others' views and beliefs, racial experiences or even freedom of speech at times. In my opinion and personal experience, these restrictions can be one of the biggest hindrances we face in society. Obviously, the *regular effect* has much to do with it.

What does this mean in layman's terms? Sometimes, you're seen as an asshole when you say what's on your mind or do things differently than society deems acceptable.

For example, when we were children in school, if we had something to say, we would put our hand up to ensure we didn't interrupt anyone. Manners, gotta love them! But if we weren't chosen, we kept whatever we had to say inside. We added zero value because we didn't share, and by the time we got home, we probably forgot what we had to say.

Expressing yourself is a big part of breaking out of social constraints. I'm a strong believer in not offending anyone or speaking out about very touchy subjects if you're not an expert or going through any of those experiences. I'm not saying that all of these restraints are bad, but when I was a child, they were a little too tight. If I was sitting in class and had something to say, sometimes I wouldn't share because I thought I would ask a "stupid" question, get made fun of, laughed at, and possibly picked on at recess. It happened all the time! We need to encourage children to speak out more often, say what's on their mind, and teach them how to be politically correct to ensure that they don't offend anyone, from a very young age.

One of the other too-tight restraints was parental. Now, don't get me wrong, I had a wonderful childhood, have amazing parents, and was raised to be a very respectful person. When I look back, there are a few things I wish I had experienced as a child; instead, I experienced them later, in university. I understand that it's hard for parents to let their children run free, but that freedom can mature and ready them for the real world at a very young age.

I noticed a change in myself when I went to university. I had the opportunity to make friends with whomever I wanted. When you're younger, your parents have control over who you spend your time with. They can tell you not to hang with this person or that person, and the reasoning I always got was "just because," which of course makes zero sense. But in university, I could write my own story about how many people I met. The entire experience was extremely refreshing because it opened up my mind to different types of people, different cultures, and different life experiences. I would have friends for years and talk about them at home, and my parents would ask so many questions about who they were. They could feel that restraint loosening, and I was loving every minute of it!

Since we're talking about parental constraints, often hear from friends and family that they would never marry someone their parents did not accept. Sometimes, they have a religious reason; often, it becomes a cultural reason. In 2018 and beyond, I say we drop the bullshit and marry whomever the heck we want. A few years ago, I probably would've thought the same. And don't get me wrong, you always want your parents to like and respect your spouse and vice versa. But does that mean you should throw away what may be the best thing to ever happen to you just because your parents are living with a few old-school traits?

The more I think about it, the less I feel the need to get permission to marry. I want to specifically discuss this topic because I've spoken to a few relationship coaches; they all say it's extremely unhealthy to fall into the trap of getting married for the sake of getting married because your parents said you have to get married—a mouthful, I know, but are you with me? Often, a couple will be in a relationship for a few years, then they break up, and a few months later, one of them is engaged to someone else. Now, this might be great! If you've found "the one," power to you. But are you instead jumping into that trap?

My parents always had a plan for me: get married, have a few kids, and live at home with them. I always joke with my mom that if she had her way, I would be married at twenty-five, have two kids already with another one on the way, and be living in her basement. She hates when I say this, but she knows it's true! The funny thing is that when I was growing up, I actually had that same plan, because it was instilled in my brain as the right thing to do. As I got a little older, and the restraints started to loosen, I realized that there was so much more I wanted to do before I got married.

It can be very scary to break out of the parental constraints. As a child, I did everything the way my parents wanted me to, which was great because, like I said before, I had a very good upbringing. Even through high school, I was scared to tell my parents some things, especially my dad. But something changed when I went to university. Suddenly, I didn't have that fear anymore. Instead, there was total, mutual respect between myself and my dad, which I cherish to this day. I would tell him almost anything (key word: *almost*), and until the end of his time, I talked to him about my career moves, my friends, the parties I went to—discussions I thought I would never have with my parents because of that fear that I grew up with. As for my mom? Nope, still a little bit of fear there. I think that's every guy and his mom!

Here's what breaking out of the parental constraints taught me: No matter what challenges I've gone through, and no matter how angry my parents were, they've always had my back. Sharing things with them actually sparked mutual respect. I learned that talking to my parents about my future could actually be a conversation instead of an argument. Lastly, sharing taught me that my parents have experienced *way* more hardships and tribulations that I have, so they can give me some amazing advice.

Growing up, you tend to think that you know everything and your parents know nothing. Granted, you may have more education than your parents on certain topics, but they have been through so much. So, here's my challenge to you. Ask your parents, or guardians, or someone you admire about their story. You will learn something new every time.

Bonus Challenge: Explain to them what the *regular effect* is, and ask them what restraints they experienced as children. Our modern-day restraints might feel like a walk in the park after hearing what they had to go through!

NOTES

"Once you become fearless, life becomes limitless."
—UNKNOWN

What were/are some of your restraints, whether parental, social, or cultural, and what are you doing to loosen that buckle?

_____
_____
_____
_____
_____
_____
_____
_____
_____
_____
_____
_____
_____
_____
_____
_____
_____

CHAPTER 4

THE DEATH OF A MENTOR

"We all die. The goal isn't to live forever.
The goal is to create something that will."
—CHUCK PALAHNIUK

IN MAY 2014, I lost the mentor I had followed since day one; I lost my father. Growing up, you laugh when your parents get hurt, because it is a rare thing to see. At least, that was my experience. Whenever Mom or Dad hit their foot on a kitchen table leg, or their head on a cupboard, I would laugh and laugh and laugh. Why? Because my parents were my superheroes, and superheroes don't get hurt. As we get older, we tend to forget one thing—our parents are getting older with us. I admit that I forgot, and went on to live life, naively thinking that my parents would be there forever.

When I got the call that my dad had passed away, I was rushing home because my sister called thirty minutes earlier telling me that he wasn't waking up. The odd part was that as soon as I saw it was her calling, I knew what the call was about.

Life has its ups and downs. What really matters is how we handle the situations that it throws at us. I am here to tell you that death is okay, because it's the one thing that every human being has in common.

Take it from me. My dad was one of my best friends. We were very close. I enjoyed talking to him about my career, what my plans were, and what I wanted to accomplish. Unfortunately for me, Dad can't give me advice anymore, but his teachings live on, and that's the legacy that he's left behind. I talk to him all the time, and it honestly helps me every single day. Some may say that's weird, but maybe those naysayers haven't been through the same situation that I or many readers have. Talking to my dad settles me down when I'm frustrated or having a bad day. It gives me an opportunity to vent, to make a joke, and most importantly, it gives me the opportunity to smile.

I mention the death of my father for a few reasons. Number one, as I said before, I want everyone to know that death is okay, despite what society tells us #TheRegularEffect. For children with two parents, we'll probably have to go through this twice. Number two, I also want everyone to know the importance of moving on. By no means am I saying to forget—I will never forget my dad or his teachings. Moving on, though, is perfectly fine. My dad was such a positive person, I know for a damn fact that he would never want me stuck in the mindset that someone has left me and I have nowhere to go.

When someone close to you passes away, you have two options: you can either go up or down. Simple as that. When my dad passed, I made a conscious decision to go up. Sounds simple, but it really isn't, and I don't expect anyone to get over a death in a weekend. As the only son, I needed to be strong for my mom and two sisters. I also consider myself lucky to have the best family on this earth, and such a huge support system. I owe every single person who helped me through that time and pushed me upward. Without them, who knows where I would be? I hope that I can be there for others, and that reading through my situation will help those in need.

When my dad passed away, here is what went through my head: What do I do now? How will I ever let him go? *Why*?

Questions one and two are valid. What are you supposed to do when someone passes away? The rule book doesn't exist to tell you what to do, and I'm not going to tell you what to do either. I will, however, tell you what I did.

The moment I lost my dad, I realized that I needed to step up as the "man of the house." The next day, I went to my condo in Toronto, grabbed my things, and headed home to be with my family. I immediately asked myself what I was supposed to do about my mom. That was the hardest part.

I can only imagine that losing a significant other is one of the hardest things you can ever go through. After all, losing a parent is supposed to happen, and we grow up somewhat prepared for it. Losing a significant other is something that you probably think will never happen. I knew that I had to spend time with my mom. Being there for my family was my number one priority, and it was definitely the right decision.

The question of *why* occurred to me once. Literally, just once. And I told myself that I would never get the answer to that question, that this was part of a higher being's plan, and not to question it. Now, I've spoken to many friends who have lost their parents, and the question of *why* always comes up, and it's a hard question to let go. But here is the brutal reality: You will *never* get the answer to that question. No matter how much research you do, no matter how much you think about it, you will never get a definite answer. I knew I'd be doing myself a disservice if I kept questioning.

Now, years after his death, I'm proud to say that I never asked that question again, even during the tough times, and I'm even prouder that I've helped others realize that it's a question we can't answer until it's our time to pass.

How will I ever move on? I can tell you that I've never really "let my dad go," nor will I ever. I think the key is to realize reality, if that makes sense. Realize that the person will no longer be there, but always keep a piece of them around you. Get my drift? My healthiest move was to understand that my dad was gone and not coming back, so I decided to live my life to make him proud. I am confident that I'm on that journey, and I cannot wait to show my dad and the rest of my family who Shiv will be five years, ten years, and twenty years from now. That's what keeps me going. The fact that I will be able to look back and say, "Dad, check this out," or "Dad, look what I've done," or the most important one, "Dad, thank you," is very exciting for me. I've consciously decided to live a life that makes my parents, family, friends, coworkers, and, hell, even acquaintances proud of me and my accomplishments.

The funny thing is that I can't remember any of the "bad times" with my dad. I have some amazing childhood memories—lots of laughter, lots of fun, and lots of awesome times with the family. But when I think of my dad, the one memory that stands out is from the day that he passed away.

I was back home for the weekend, and Dad wanted to paint the house for my sister's wedding, which was approaching in a few months. It was a Friday night, and I went into my parents' room and told them that I didn't want to paint because I was tired from working all week long (what a lame excuse). I woke up very early on Saturday morning and something told me to change my mind. I went straight to Tim Hortons (his favorite breakfast joint) and got myself and my dad coffee and breakfast. We started painting and we had the most fantastic day. We laughed, we had a few heart-to-hearts, and we even shared a beer or two.

Funny story about the beer—my mom has *never* given me a beer, and that day, she went in the fridge and actually handed me one! Dad and I had such a great time because we did a few things that were out of the norm. My dad loved music but never liked when I played it loudly. For some reason, we blasted the music that day.

My dad was singing along and dancing, and I was so happy to see that. A few hours later, we finished painting, cleaned up, and I left for Toronto. I remember seeing my dad sleeping in his bed, and to be honest, he may have already passed away by then, I just didn't catch it. I remember looking at him and laughing because he looked so tired. I went downstairs and told Mom that Dad had worked hard that day, and he was so tired. I left Brampton and got a call about an hour later from my sister telling me that Dad wasn't waking up. I knew right then and there that he was gone, but it was hard to believe until I actually saw him when I got back home.

Sometimes life throws these situations at you. My fondest memory of my dad was the day he passed away, because I got to spend it with him. His last day on this earth was spent with his son, and that's a memory I will always cherish.

The point of my personal story is to be thankful for the memories you have with your parents. Many of you still have yours, and if you do, find a few memories that you can flick back to. They really empower you in a tough time. We all fight with our family and friends—that's normal—but find the happy memories and store them somewhere in the brain bank! Revert back to them and I guarantee that a smile will appear on your face.

Gratitude is one of the hardest traits to learn. Even now, I don't fully understand it. I try to show gratitude for my career, my family, my friends, and almost everything around me every day. I tell everyone that I learned how to be grateful the day that my dad passed away, and if I had known how to be grateful earlier, maybe he and I would have had an even better relationship. To this day, I know that my strength to break out of the *regular effect* came from my Dad—one of the most irregular people I knew. Below is a picture of me with my hero, the greatest mentor I've ever had, who is somehow still mentoring me: my dad.

NOTES

"The fear of death follows from the fear of life.
A man who lives fully is prepared to die at any time."
—MARK TWAIN

CHAPTER 5

THE IMPORTANCE OF BRANDING

"Your brand is what people say about you when you're not in the room."
—JEFF BEZOS

YOUR BRAND IS what defines you, hands down, no questions asked.

Put yourself in this situation. Let's say you work at a pharmaceutical sales company. You're currently a junior account manager, but you have an opportunity to become a senior account manager. You get into the interview and you do a great job, you say all the right things, and your sales numbers as a junior account manager are right where they should be. Do you think that's all the hiring manager considers before giving you the chance to take that next step in your career?

Nine times out of ten, I would say no. If your numbers are in the right spot, but you don't possess a good brand, and you're up against someone who has all the right relationships with the stakeholders in your company but lower numbers, they will get the job before you, and that's just the reality of it. We can all agree that the best place to be is the person with great sales and a great brand. Sometimes you can't have both—choose the great brand, and strive for the great sales. A great brand will get you further, not just in the company, but in your own personal life. If you have a better brand, your sales will probably increase because your customers will love you. They will no longer see you as just a salesman, they will see you as a human being.

Some people forget that the words they speak are part of their brand. If you go back on your word, you are doing a disservice to your personal brand. As one of my virtual mentors (as I like to call him), Tim Ferris, says, "A good personal brand shouldn't be the goal; it should be a side-effect of having good goals and acting consistently."

I wholeheartedly agree with Ferris's statement. Building a brand isn't really a goal; however, the goals that you set along the way will help you build it, and what you say will add to it, if you stick to your word! It's one of the hardest things to do, but people will *always*, and I repeat, *always* remember the time you went back on your word or broke your promise. People often prioritize the bad times over the good times, so it's your duty to ensure that your promises are kept.

The big man himself, Tony Robbins, is a great role model when it comes to branding. He says, "As you add more to your brand, your whole world will expand . . . the strongest force in the human personality is the need to stay consistent with how we define ourselves."

I couldn't have put that better myself. Although the words of Tim Ferris and Tony Robbins sound different, they intertwine quite well. Ferris talks about not setting your brand as a goal, but instead working towards the goals to define your brand. Robbins states the importance of staying consistent with how we define ourselves and our brand. If our goals remain consistent, our brand will be defined.

Let me put this into perspective. If I'm at work, and my goal is to become the regional manager, I would start to change the way I think and the way I portray myself. We've all heard the expression, "If you can walk the walk you can talk the talk." That summarizes what Robbins is saying, and setting the goal of becoming a regional manager is what Ferris is talking about. Regardless of the goal, I will tailor myself to reach it, which is adding to my own personal brand. You must be adaptive to change when searching for your future role. Sometimes, you may need to change the way you communicate in order to be taken more seriously. Sometimes, you may need to dress differently. This is all part of the branding game. Are you ready to play?

Here's what I'd like you to do. In the space below, write down the five most important traits that you currently possess, and five goals that you would like to work on. The point of this exercise is to put your traits and goals side by side so that you can see how they work together.

	TRAITS	GOALS
1.		
2.		
3.		
4.		
5.		

Some of your goals may be to become a millionaire by age thirty, build an orphanage, or own a fancy car or house in the near future. All of those are great goals, but you need to possess the correct traits in order to achieve them. Take a look at what you've written above. Can you see how they intertwine?

The importance of branding comes up in daily conversation for me. Branding has a lot to do with what's politically correct, respectful, and real. Being politically correct to an extent is a big chunk of your brand. Political correctness shows awareness of your surroundings, and ensures that you're not using language or gestures that offend a particular person or group. Whether you like it or not, people are going to judge and rate you based on how you think and how you come across. Your brand should cater to your conception of the public or the people around you.

I'm not saying to change you who are, but you're allowed to tweak yourself based on your audience. If you go against what the general population says or agrees with, sometimes your brand can be gone like the wind, diminished in a matter of minutes. Being politically correct is a smart move when branding yourself because it allows you to feel out your target audience.

Respect is another large piece of the puzzle, and this goes hand-in-hand with being politically correct. When creating your personal brand, be sure to respect everyone, including your competition. I see certain individuals create their company and start bashing their competition right away. Personally, I lose respect for them. The world needs competition, and there are other ways to win. Respecting other peoples' views is very important, and you can learn a thing or two if you just keep that window open. If you debut to the world but are disrespectful in your manner, you will be disregarded quickly.

Working on my personal branding and meeting people from all walks of life has taught me one thing—there are more good people in the world than bad. More people will walk away if you disrespect them or a certain group. Keep that in mind when creating a brand for yourself, and think about how you will be perceived by different people.

I support political correctness, but I also believe that being "real" is another huge weapon in the branding arsenal. I'm sure I am not the first to say this, but in today's society, it seems as though people are offended by the slightest things. The *regular effect* has made it almost impossible to be honest or upfront with anyone about any given subject. Being who you truly are can offend people. Deal with it. If you can tweak your messaging about who you are to the world, then I would suggest that. But if you have to do a complete 180-degree turn to properly brand, then what's the point? You obviously don't stand for it, or are not passionate about it, so why create a "fake" personal brand?

Here's a real-life example: As I explain elsehwere, I used to weigh quite a lot. I started training after I lost the weight with the hopes that people would be motivated by my change. This totally worked! I was helping a lot of people lose weight and get fit (and most of them have bypassed my fitness levels, so I have some catching up to do!). Some, however, were not too happy when I told them that they needed to change their diet, or find time. Some individuals were extremely offended that I would call them out on what they ate for breakfast or on Facebook pictures from the night before of them swigging down eight beers.

In this particular situation, I didn't care if I was offending people. I truly believe that if you want to help yourself, you need to make that decision. If you're not willing to accept your wrongdoings or do what's necessary to make a change, then I can no longer help you. And if you're offended because *you* are not willing to change your habits when I'm taking time out of *my* day to help you, then I really don't care to invest my time with you.

This would be a hard conversation to have with many

close friends and family members. People got offended because I was telling them what I used to do. I've walked in their shoes. Who better to take advice from than someone who's already walked that path? In certain situations, offense was taken because those individuals hadn't woken up yet, and I think it's important to say that I used to be exactly where they were.

With all that being said, the message here is to be yourself. Your brand is you, so *own* it. I never recommend stepping out of the *true you* to fit what society wants you to be. Let me break that down. Most people walk in a straight line. Why? Because that's what is socially accepted. I, for one, choose to go left or right. The straight line isn't me, so I am usually myself in most situations. I do understand that certain times call for a certain type of behavior, and I'm all for that. But to change the way you truly are just to fit in with society? That's a *hell no* for Shiv.

I truly admire people who have everything but do not flaunt it. These individuals are so humble that they are too shy to show off. When you peel the onion back a bit, what are their core values? Probably to help people. That's the correlation I make. Right away, I make the association between their personal brand and their willingness to help people. Being humble is a great branding trait to possess because it shows that you're genuine and willing to help the person next to you. These types of people are exactly who they were before the fame and riches. The fact that they have stayed the same after a huge life change is extremely admirable, and we have so much to learn from these types of people.

NOTES

"If people like you, they will listen to you. But if they trust you,
they will do business with you."
—ZIG ZIGLAR

_____
_____
_____
_____
_____
_____
_____
_____
_____
_____
_____
_____
_____
_____
_____
_____
_____

CHAPTER 6

SHOP 'TILL YOU DROP—THE POWER OF NETWORKING

> "Know where you want to go and
> make sure the right people know about it."
> **—MEREDITH MAHONEY**

IN CHAPTER 5, WE talked about the importance of your brand, and how setting the correct goals will define your brand. This chapter talks about the power of networking, and believe it or not, your personal brand has a lot to do with building your network. Let's take a look at some stats first:

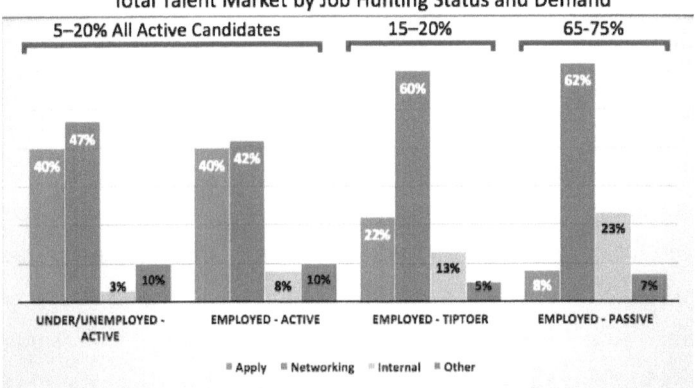

This graph speaks *volumes*. As you can see, networking wins the race and then some. We touched on the importance of branding, and how a negative brand can block you from moving to the next step in your career. My advice to every person on *Earth* can be summarized in three words: network, network, and . . . network.

Networking is like window shopping. You don't actually need to buy anything, but you need to look at what you can have, and maybe take ideas, go home, and try to recreate what you saw. Networking is the exact same thing (maybe without the Gucci dress shoes). When you network and get

---

1 [https://www.linkedin.com/pulse/new-survey-reveals-85-all-jobs-filled-via-networking-lou-adler]

to know someone, you are listening to their experiences, listening to how they got to where they are, and even taking some of their ideas and making them your own. You are building a relationship with them, much like building a relationship with a brand when you buy something from their store.

When you shop, you sometimes realize that you don't actually like the product or service. In the world of networking, you will not like everyone you meet, and may not take the advice of numerous people. Filtering knowledge and information is key. Some people may give you the worst pessimistic advice, and some may give you the advice you need to get your business started. Make sure you filter out the bullshit and really understand what's crucial. Nothing is wrong with adopting as your own the personality traits of those you respect. We all do it when we see the likes of Tim Cook or Tony Robbins speak to an audience. Although we may not be fond of every trait, we can pick and choose the traits we'd like to improve on.

Networking has a lot to do with getting out of your comfort zone, which we have talked about quite a bit in this book. To properly network, there are some key tips that I hope you find useful.

My first tip is to join LinkedIn, an online, social networking service that is tailored to business professionals in almost every industry. My experience on LinkedIn has been phenomenal, opening many doors to meet the people I have needed, whether it is in my job or my personal life.

Another healthy tip is to join social groups at work. "But Shiv, what if my work doesn't have a social group?" Great question, oh brave one. Go and create one. You be the boss, you make the decisions, you pick the tasks. Not only will you create your own social team, you will be taking charge and probably stepping outside of your comfort zone! Becoming a part of these groups not only connects you with like-minded people, it opens your mind to different ideas that may help you discover your next business idea. It also gives you the opportunity to try something new—to change your approach when talking to people. You may be used to a "regular" approach, but now you can essentially re-invent yourself when meeting a new set of people.

Does anyone else hate those awkward elevator rides where you're stuck with six other people from floor one to twenty-seven and no one makes a sound? Everyone is on their phones despite there not being any reception, and no one makes eye contact? Seriously, what are people looking at?!

This is where I shine. I make it a point, every single day, to break the norm. It's regular for an elevator of people who do not know each other to be silent. To that I say, "Make some damn noise!" It's a simple task to say "Hello" or "Good morning" or "Nice shoes." That is my challenge to you. Not only does it break the awkward silence, but you are now in control of the conversation. This is forcing you to come out of your comfort zone, and you are helping others by removing them from their own. Double whammy!

I find this to be a very simple but extremely important task. With that being said, I am guilty of breaking this rule. Sometimes even I find it tough to break that awkward silence, especially when there is no expression on anyone's face other than the classic *get-me-out-of-here* look.

There is a quote that I really enjoy: "When you meet a man without a smile, give him one of yours." Simple, yet powerful. If you see someone without a smile, just smile at them. Nine times out of ten, you will probably get one back. It's like the old trick of fake laughing. If you start to fake laugh with someone, the chances are that it will turn into a real laugh—unless it starts to get creepy, then my advice is to stop immediately! There's nothing like an old elevator pitch to show someone who you are, which is the person in control.

NOTES

"A simple hello could lead to a million things."
—UNKNOWN

CHAPTER 7

EXCUSES, EXCUSES, EXCUSES

> "The first step to getting anywhere is deciding you're not willing to stay where you are."
> **—UNKNOWN**

A FEW YEARS ago, I made a conscious decision to do something that would change my life, and that was to lose some serious weight. Here is a picture of me at my heaviest.

While some may argue that I look extremely happy (any joke can make me laugh, even the worst ones!), I was very unhappy. Growing up, I was always very fit. My parents enrolled me in martial arts at a very young age. I excelled in Tae Kwon Do (shout-out to the team at Master's Tae Kwon Do!) and learned many of its core values.

After about twelve years, I stopped attending Master's. I went off to high school and college and ate everything in sight. Before I knew it, I went from 130 pounds in grade eight to almost 300 pounds in college. Think about it. The time span was only five to six years! That was a 170-pound weight gain in a short amount of time.

I was teased during my college years by a few close friends. My mind wasn't where it once was. I grew up with confidence, but by college it was nowhere to be found, hidden inside of me. Then I met someone to whom I attribute my weight loss: Yasir Rana. Although I hate telling him, because he loves the credit, he did really push me into the gym, which in turn changed my life for the better.

Around the age of twenty, I woke up one morning with chest pains. I visited the doctor at the walk-in clinic, and after waiting a few hours, he finally saw me. I was in and out of that doctor's office in about five minutes. He checked my blood pressure, checked my heart rate, and looked at me and told me that I needed to lose weight or I would probably die by the time I was thirty. As a twenty-year-old who thought he knew everything, I stormed out of that doctor's office and headed to the nearest KFC, my go-to choice for comfort food.

As I sat there with my three-piece meal, fries, and gravy, I remember being angry at the doctor, thinking, "How could he tell his patient that he's fat. Who does he think he is?" I was extremely angry, but the KFC calmed me down. I went home, went to bed, and that was that.

The next morning, I woke up and thought about it all over again. I didn't want to die when I was thirty. Hell, my life hadn't even started yet. There was a track behind a high school close to my house, so I decided to throw on some gym attire and head to the track. I would walk for ten minutes and run for thirty seconds, then walk for ten minutes, then run for thirty seconds. After a few days, I would walk for nine minutes, and run for forty-five seconds.

It doesn't seem like a long time, but for a twenty-year-old pushing 290 pounds, I was extremely happy to be moving. I tried to do better and better, and I would gradually move to walking less and running more. A few weeks later, I even challenged my friends to come with me. They obviously did a lot better than me in terms of running, but the experience made me want to do even better. At the time, I had one competitor, and that was myself—the regular, large guy in the mirror.

Over the next eleven months, I stopped drinking alcohol, stopped eating fast food, and started to really take my health seriously. I even stopped going out with friends, because I knew that it was a sacrifice that would soon pay off. I lost 145 pounds in 11 months.

Now, here is the question I'm asked all the time: "Was it hard?" To be honest, the answer is no. If you want to lose weight and get healthier, the only person stopping you is yourself. I say to stop being lazy, and I think I've earned the right to call you out! People frequently ask me for help and tips to lose weight. Many do not go to the gym or do anything active. Those are the people I stop giving advice to. If you tell me you have no time, I will call you a liar. If you tell me you're too tired after work, I will call you lazy. But if you tell me you can't do it, I'm here to tell you that *you can*.

All in all, the excuses need to be written on a piece of paper, crushed into a ball, and tossed into the garbage, Kobe-style. What do you think is the biggest excuse I hear as to why people can't lose weight? You've probably guessed it already: time. Time is always the first excuse. People tell me that they don't have time to go to the gym in the morning, or don't have time to get active after work, or can't do anything active during the day.

All I do is smile and say, "Everybody has the same

twenty-four hours in the day." Sometimes, I even walk away after saying it to add a dramatic effect. It doesn't matter who you are, you can find twenty to thirty minutes a day to do something active. Whether you are taking the stairs at work, walking to the grocery store instead of driving, or even doing a short home workout, your health should always be your number one priority. If Barack Obama found time to work out for five to six hours a week during his presidency, I'm fairly certain you can find half of that time in your week to break a sweat or two.

One of the most rewarding feelings I get isn't from knowing that I dropped the weight—it's the fact that I've helped many people with their weight-loss journey, whether I'm coaching them through it at the gym, or motivating them from afar as they creep my Facebook or Instagram (I encourage you to do so!). If I can help you in any way to meet your fitness goals, I urge you to send me an email (shiv@shivrad.com), and I will get back to you. Sometimes, all you need is a nudge from someone who actually did it instead of someone who's been fit all their life! Let me be that guy; let me give you the nudge that you need.

Remember, there is no invisible wall; there is no glass ceiling. Take it from a "regular" guy who always thought there was. The only thing in front of you is a big, huge excuse—it's your decision whether or not you want it to go away. There will always be something "stopping" you from working out, but I think every person can spare twenty to thirty minutes a day to do something active. If not twenty minutes, then make it fifteen, but you have to move and get your blood flowing in order to lose weight.

Make time. Wake up thirty minutes earlier, go to bed twenty minutes later, hit the gym on your lunch break, put the burgers down and pick up a salad. It's a very easy conscious decision to make—you just have to want it that badly! If you're tired of being a regular person, challenge yourself to do something you wouldn't normally do. If getting active is out of the norm, try it out. You're not just working out physically; you're working out mentally.

Losing the weight didn't just help me physically, it helped me mentally. It gave me a shovel to dig deep and find that confidence I always knew I had, that confidence that was buried deep inside. My weight loss gave me my confidence back, and I wouldn't have it any other way.

I thought it would be important to add some structure and content as to exactly what I did to drop the pounds. It's true what they say, diet is almost 70%-80% of the magic, but I realized that if I wanted to speed up the process, I needed to add some cardio into my daily routine.

Here's an old weekly plan that I found and followed for 11 months (not much detail, but it's a kick-start):

DAYS	DIET	EXCERSISE	NOTES
1	**Breakfast:** 2 eggs, bowl of fruit, oatmeal **Lunch:** Salmon, salad (no dressing), nuts (non-salted), avocado **Dinner:** Lean chicken breast, salad, brown rice, fruit	**Morning exercise:** Stretching, 2k-4k run followed by more stretching **Evening exercise:** Follow daily weight program of choice, 30 mins of cardio post-weight training Change workout routine monthly (Follow one plan for one month, then change)	Change workout routine monthly (Follow one plan for one month, then change) Snack on nuts, protein shakes (no milk, only water)
2	**Breakfast:** 2 eggs, cereal with skim milk **Lunch:** Salmon, salad (no dressing), nuts (non-salted), avocado **Dinner:** Salmon, salad, brown rice, fruit	**Morning exercise:** Stretching, 2k-4k run followed by more stretching **Evening exercise:** Follow daily weight program of choice, 30 mins of cardio post-weight training	Change workout routine monthly (Follow one plan for one month, then change) Snack on nuts, protein shakes (no milk, only water)
3	**Breakfast:** 2 eggs, bowl of fruit, oatmeal **Lunch:** Salmon, salad (no dressing), nuts (non-salted), avocado **Dinner:** Lean chicken breast, salad, brown rice, fruit	**REST DAY** (Light stretching or cardio)	Snack on nuts, protein shakes (no milk, only water)

4	**Breakfast:** Oatmeal, bowl of fruit x 2 **Lunch:** Salmon, salad (no dressing), nuts (non-salted), avocado **Dinner:** Salmon, salad, brown rice, fruit	**Morning exercise:** Stretching, 2k-4k run followed by more stretching **Evening exercise:** Follow daily weight program of choice, 30 mins of cardio post-weight training	Change workout routine monthly (Follow one plan for one month, then change) Snack on nuts, protein shakes (no milk, only water)
5	**Breakfast:** 2 eggs, bowl of fruit, oatmeal **Lunch:** Salmon, salad (no dressing), nuts (non-salted), avocado **Dinner:** Lean chicken breast, salad, brown rice, fruit	**Morning exercise:** Stretching, 2k-4k run followed by more stretching **Evening exercise:** Follow daily weight program of choice, 30 mins of cardio post-weight training	Change workout routine monthly (Follow one plan for one month, then change) Snack on nuts, protein shakes (no milk, only water)
6	**Breakfast:** 4 egg whites, bowl of fruit **Lunch:** Salmon, salad (no dressing), nuts (non-salted), avocado **Dinner:** Salmon, salad, brown rice, fruit	**Morning exercise:** Stretching, 2k-4k run followed by more stretching **Evening exercise:** Follow daily weight program of choice, 30 mins of cardio post-weight training	Change workout routine monthly (Follow one plan for one month, then change) Snack on nuts, protein shakes (no milk, only water)
7	**Breakfast:** 2 eggs, bowl of fruit, oatmeal **Lunch:** Salmon, salad (no dressing), nuts (non-salted), avocado **Dinner:** Lean chicken breast, salad, brown rice, fruit	**REST DAY** (Light stretching or cardio)	Change workout routine monthly (Follow one plan for one month, then change) Snack on nuts, protein shakes (no milk, only water)

This meal plan may seem a bit plain, but it did the trick! A few extra pointers. Try to limit alcohol consumption, as well as sugar. Sugar was my main cause for the weight gain, and when majority was cut from my diet, I started to shed the pounds right away. ***Keep in mind that you can still consume your chocolate, coffee and indulge in other scrumptious foods, but consistency is key, and so is portion. Limit as much as you can, but remember that it's okay to have a bit of fun. Just ensure you make your workouts count.

NOTES

"I may not be there yet, but I'm closer than I was yesterday."
—JOSÉ N. HARRIS

What are some of your fitness goals? Write them here to make them real!

_____
_____
_____
_____
_____
_____
_____
_____
_____
_____
_____
_____
_____
_____
_____
_____

CHAPTER 8

THE BEST MEDICINE IN THE CABINET: LAUGHTER

"Always laugh when you can. It is cheap medicine."
—LORD BYRON

THESE DAYS, YOU'RE prescribed medicine for practically everything. If you're feeling down, here are some pills. If you're coughing, here are more pills. If your feet hurt, here are some pain meds, suck 'em down.

I'm here to prescribe you something that gets me through every single day: laughter. Why is laughter important? Laughter can increase your mood ten-fold. It can get rid of your fears, make you forget the bad times, and even introduce you to new friends. Keep the people and things that make you smile and laugh close to you. A life without laughter is a very dark life. Imagine going a week straight without laughing or smiling. Some people live their lives like that. I dedicate my life to making people crack a smile. A smile can tell a thousand stories, and I consider it an honour to be a part of it.

Although I'm far away from many of my close friends—most of them in Toronto—I always make it a point to reach out and say hi. Why? Because my friends bring me happiness and laughter. We're a fun bunch that has experienced so much together. It's always worth bringing up an old memory for the sake of a few laughs. Try to find what brings you laughter, and stay in arm's reach. Everyone has bad days. Shit happens. What really defines you is how you crawl out of the dark side (yes, another *Star Wars* reference!) and into the light.

Shiv, why are you talking about your friends?! How are they going to help me?! The answer is simple. Join us. And I say that because I truly mean it. The reason my group of friends and I get along with everyone is because we're an open bunch. In fact, my entire group of close friends doesn't let the *regular effect* deter them from chasing their dreams, and that is refreshing to see.

Which brings me to the topic of openness—being open to new relationships, meeting new people, and developing new connections. As I stated before, when I moved to Australia, I knew two people. *Two* people in the entire country. The fear of having zero friends was a real struggle, but my willingness to be open was a "major key" (thanks DJ Khaled!).

If I were close-minded, what good would that do? Seriously? I wouldn't be liked at work, I wouldn't have met anyone, and I wouldn't have experienced many of the things I've done here in Australia. Laughter helps me be more open-minded. It allows me to use my imagination a bit more. The reason laughter is such a huge subject to me is because I make it a big part of my everyday life. No matter what, I will either laugh or make someone else laugh—which usually ends up with me laughing even more than them. Why? Because I genuinely think laughter is a cure for mild depression.

Here's my example. I was sitting on my couch in Sydney watching clips on YouTube, and I was heading down a negative slope. I was in a shaky relationship with my now-ex-girlfriend from Toronto. I thought about what I should do and how I should handle the situation. I was wondering who I could speak to; I never go to my family for these things, and my friends, quite frankly, were tired of hearing about it.

I was going deeper and deeper into the darkness. Was that depression? I'm not sure, but for the first time in my life, I was thinking about how the world would be without me, and if it would be easier if I just . . . disappeared. I was angry at myself. I am generally a positive person, but it was a dark time. What happened next is exactly why I consider laughter a cure.

Have you heard of JusReign? He's a comedian from Brampton, Canada, where I was born and raised. JusReign, a.k.a. Jasmeet Singh, is a young, talented individual whose job is to make people laugh. Let me tell you this—he does his job very well. After sitting on the couch thinking about my next steps, I put on YouTube, went to JusReign's page, and started watching his videos.

I never laughed so hard in my life. I laughed so hard that I cried. I don't think I was crying because he was so funny—I think I was crying out of happiness that I had crawled out of that dark place and back into the light. Those videos took me out of the worst spot of my life, and I cherish that memory as well.

JusReign, if you're reading this, we met once outside of Osmows (of course) and that was it, but you've had a *huge* impact on my life, and you're doing this through your videos. If you're helping me with my life, you're definitely helping others. This is a big *thank you*. Thanks for doing what you do. You are a role model to the younger generation, and a motivational idol for the rest, including yours truly.

Nowadays, whenever I'm feeling sad, angry, or just in a bad spot, I do something that helps me get out of it. I encourage all of you to make a noise, say something, or do something that will help you. Want to know what I do? I snap my fingers. It's as simple as that. I snap my fingers and say three words, "Change your state." Let me tell you, this shit works, and I'd be happy for you to use it. I took it from the big man himself, Tony Robbins. It's funny what you can do when you give yourself permission to do it. When

I snap my fingers, it's like I'm giving myself permission to snap out of the poor situation that I'm in, and get back to being the positive Shiv that I am and love. It really works, and I encourage all of you to try it.

The first time I did it, it didn't work because I didn't believe it in. Put some faith into these little phrases and sayings, and you'll be surprised at what you can achieve by even the simplest gesture.

Write down a few things that make you laugh. Is it a friend, family member, or a memory? Put them on paper and make them real so you can refer back to them when you're in a bad spot:

_____
_____
_____
_____
_____
_____
_____
_____

Feel better? Refer to these whenever you are feeling down. I write things down that make me laugh all the time, and the best thing is that they keep changing. When I write them down, they become real memories. I refer to them and keep these memories fresh in my mind instead of letting the moment be whisked away by the wind.

Another reason why laughter is so important to me is because I enjoy hearing other people laugh. Do you ever get the urge to smile when you hear laughter, even when you don't even know what's funny? No? Is that just me . . . ?

Now, don't get me wrong, I'm no Russell Peters, but I've been told that I'm a tad witty at times—from my family, of course. I absolutely hate to be serious all the time. Yes, being serious is sometimes the right way to go, but a little giggle never hurt anybody! I like to think that I help people when I make them laugh. When I'm around my family and we're having fun, that is one of the best feelings ever. I challenge you to get out there and try to make someone laugh every single day. It can be a random person in the elevator, or your boss, or your girlfriend or boyfriend. Whoever it may be, try it for a week, email me, and let me know how you do.

Why are you encouraging me to make strangers laugh, Shiv? Isn't that creepy? Some may argue a big fat *yes*, but do you remember what this book is about? Society has taught us that to be regular, we stay quiet during office hours, laughing is a negative because too much laughter in the office is unprofessional, and that you shouldn't speak to strangers in the elevator; otherwise, you're being weird! The *regular effect* holds us hostage in our own minds.

I think you already know my answer to that bull, so again, take the challenge and tell me how it goes. I say a number of things to random people, and sometimes it's as easy as complimenting them. Seven times out of ten, you at least get a smile, and you have to smile before you laugh!

I have a 70-percent success rate—sometimes people just think I'm flirting with them, and other times I'll get the cold shoulder mixed with the eye-roll. I call that "The Regular Effect: Pissed Off, Volume 1."

Please take the challenge seriously. Again, I encourage you to find something that makes you laugh every day. Whether it's a video on YouTube, a meme on Instagram, or a conversation with a friend or family member, make it a point to visit that every single day. Make someone laugh in the process and I promise that you will enjoy this challenge a lot more.

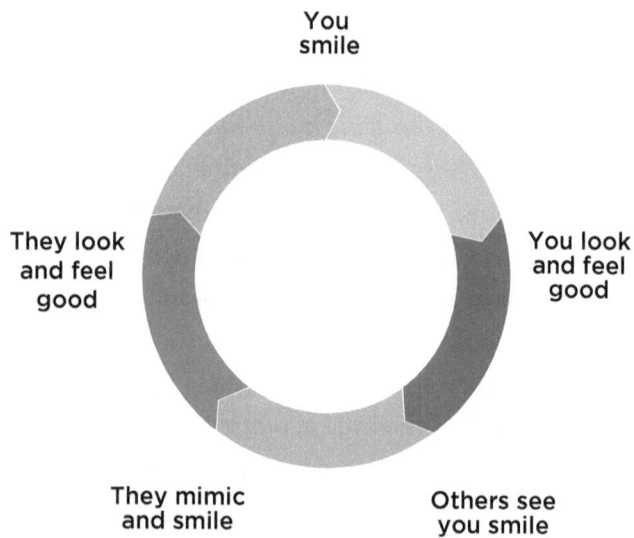

NOTES

"A day without laughter is a day wasted."
—CHARLIE CHAPLIN

CHAPTER 9

PROTECTING YOUR ENTHUSIASM

"Surround yourself with people that reflect who you want to be and how you want to feel. Energies are contagious."
—RACHEL WOLCHIN

I THOUGHT FOR a few weeks about how to actually put the topic of this chapter on paper. I thought about leaving it out of the book for this one reason: It will offend quite a few people. Guess what I did next? Snapped my fingers, said, "Change your state," and started writing.

Why is protecting your enthusiasm so important, and how do I protect mine? I'm going to tell you exactly how I do it. But first, what does protecting your enthusiasm really mean? What needs to be protected here?

Your enthusiasm defines you. Whether you are speaking, being quiet, sitting, standing, walking, or running, your enthusiasm oozes out of your body and creates either a positive or negative ambiance around you. I think of it as my own protective shield—a force field, if you will. No matter what situation I am in, and no matter who I'm around, I always choose to keep that positive force field around me. It's almost like taking your best friend around with you everywhere you go! Quite frankly, your best friend is yourself.

One of the ways I protect my enthusiasm and positivity is by "trimming the fat." By this, I mean cutting loose the negative people. This is by far one of the toughest things you will probably ever have to do, but your life will be a lot better for it. It's like seeing a new light at the end of the tunnel. I've successfully limited the number of negative people in my life, and it's the best thing I have done. People who are negative towards you, your goals, your past achievements, and even your general take on life need to be cut off from your force field. Get them out of there and never let them back in.

It's an exercise I've completed in the past year. These negative people can be your close friends and even your own family members! My advice is to gradually push them out of that force field, so you can finally focus on your goals without a shadow cast over you. My goals, ideas, and thoughts have been shunned by the people I kept close to me until I realized that they were just the wrong people. I am not saying that you should stop talking to these people outright—that's tough for anyone to do. Keep them far enough that they can't cast that shadow. See the light, and you'll never go back.

One of the major changes I made was surrounding myself with like-minded, positive people who have equally positive force fields. Telling the difference between a positive and a negative person is easy. It's amazing the things you can accomplish when you surround yourself with people who have similar goals to you. When everyone has the same positive attitude, the sky's the limit. Can you imagine going from a very dark place to one filled with lights bright enough to need sunglasses? That's what the change feels like!

In the past year or so, I've surrounded myself with people who complement me as a human being: people who are out there to help the world, and people who are so focused on helping others that they don't mind letting you in their force field for a while. This is such a refreshing feeling, and I would love for you all to experience it. Onwards and upwards—that's the only way to go.

My advice to you? Open up your force field to people you can learn from, but more importantly, people you can teach. If you are willing to help others and teach them the rights and wrongs of your experiences, you're already ten steps ahead of the game. The willingness to share information these days is rare, but it's our job and, dare I say, our obligation to change that. What's the point of hiding secrets? Wouldn't you rather share your success with your friends than climb the ladder by yourself?

Why is the ability to teach so important? For many reasons. For starters, I truly believe that repeating what I've been taught over the years equips me to be more effective in whatever I'm doing. It's like learning how to drive. The more you practice, the better you get, and the better you can maneuver through the traffic (a.k.a. bullshit) and know when to speed up or slow down.

The willingness to educate others, maybe those who are new in their business venture, allows you to share your *dos and don'ts* with them. If you can stop them from traveling down a dark road to failure, wouldn't you rather tell them? In some cases, people need to "learn the hard way," and I'm not saying to feed them with a silver spoon instead, but pointing them in the right direction is very gratifying.

Protecting your enthusiasm protects your personality. Sometimes, the closest people to you will be your toughest critics, which is needed. But sometimes they are actually the ones bringing you down. The *regular effect* possesses every single person, and it can teach us selfishness. If you break out of the *effect*, you quickly realize who has your best interest in mind, who is tagging along, and who wants to see you fail. Word of advice? Keep only those who have the best interest in your success as a person. Cut the rest loose, distance yourself, and watch how much advancement you will make in your first three months outside the negative shadow. *Protect. Your. Force field.*

NOTES

"You're a product of your environment.
Surround yourself with the best."
—JACO GERRITS

_____
_____
_____
_____
_____
_____
_____
_____
_____
_____
_____
_____
_____
_____
_____
_____
_____
_____
_____
_____

CHAPTER 10

EVEN ALI HAD A MENTOR

> "Mentoring is a brain to pick, ears to listen, and a push in the right direction."
> **—JOHN C. CROSBY**

MENTORSHIP IS ONE of the sharpest tools in the belt. I touch on mentorship many times because it plays such a huge part in my life. As I stated previously, I have over ten mentors at any given time—some that I share a lot of similarities with and some with whom I have nothing in common. I give credit to each and every one of them. My success so far has a lot to do with the mentors I surround myself with, and the people I attach myself to. It's amazing how many mentors you can have at once, and equally as amazing who they can be. My parents, first and foremost, were my mentors growing up. They still mentor me, but I realized that I couldn't get all the information I needed from them, so I started reaching out to other people I could learn from. That's another of the best decisions I ever made.

The old Shiv thought he knew everything. Now that I've been exposed to so many experiences, I've realized (pretty damn quickly) that there is so much more to learn in this world. It's important to remember that everyone you meet knows something that you don't, so don't forget to open your ears and listen. So many questions were answered because I spoke to the right people, and those answers also derived a thousand more questions.

This is why it's very important to keep these mentors in your life. I still speak to each of my mentors. We not only learn from each other, but we've developed great relationships along the way. Keeping in contact with these mentors is a priority, since I'm trying to balance so many different things in my life #juggler. My mentors point me in the right direction, whether I'm making a business or personal decision.

I know what you're thinking: with ten-plus mentors, doesn't their advice get diluted? Not really. Some mentors I only reach out to for business advice, some for personal advice, and some just to have a great conversation. Just because over ten people give you opinions doesn't mean you have to follow them; gathering opinions just means that you respect and value them.

Many of my mentors are the complete opposite of me. I can be loud (at times . . . most of the time . . . all of the time), and I used to search for mentors who were exactly the same as me. I would make sure that our passions aligned, our personalities matched, and even made sure our life experiences were somewhat the same. That was great, but I realized that something was missing. It's like dating someone who is the exact same as you. It can get boring! Always doing the same thing, seeing things in the same light, and never having a dispute on perspective.

Finding a mentor is like looking for the next date. You're more interested when that person has a different personality, has a different life story, and has experienced some things you haven't. That sounds like an ideal date to me! They may notice something you haven't because you're too blinded by a part to see the whole.

Some of my mentors are extremely quiet, and our phone calls are the quickest calls ever. I might ask a question, and the answer will either be a "yes" or a "no," and we will move on to the next topic.

Once, when I thought of a "mentor," I imagined an older gentleman. In my early days, especially in university, I always reached out to older males for mentorship. Today, I'm proud to say that almost half of my mentors are women. They range from women around my age or older. By far this has been one of the best decisions I have ever made. Sometimes women see things men can't, and men see things women can't. Mix up your mentors! Ensure you have mentors from different races, genders, careers, and age brackets.

Quite a few of my mentors are younger than me. *Yes*, it is possible to learn from younger people! One mentor is a few years younger. Another mentor, a younger gentleman, is probably one of my top mentors for any sort of business idea that I have—I make sure he's one of the first people that I call. Opening the door to different types of mentors is so important because everyone has a different perspective on things. It's imperative that you get as much information as you can when you're about to make a big decision. Different mentors will make your decision well-rounded.

Who are some of your mentors? Write them down here. If you don't have any, think of a few people you can reach out to for mentorship:

_____
_____
_____
_____
_____
_____
_____
_____

Make it a point to reach out if you haven't already. You'll be surprised at how many people genuinely like to help others.

Think of mentorship as having your very own board of directors. This panel benefits from you doing well because they get the satisfaction of knowing that they have helped. You can also bring these mentors into your business ideas if they are open to it. Mentors get to know you personally and as a business person. They know your strengths and weaknesses.

I tend to have mentors who help me fine-tune my strengths, and other mentors who work with me to strengthen my weaknesses.

It's amazing how quickly a weakness can become a strength. A huge fear of mine used to be public speaking. I would literally tremble when I was in front of an audience, and in front of an audience and couldn't find my words. When I was in my comfort zone, I was actually a pretty good speaker, so I worked with a mentor who helped me tweak the way I thought about public speaking. Today, I'm proud to say that public speaking is a hobby of mine. It's very refreshing to see how far I've come, and it was my mentor giving me that little kick in the ass that jumpstarted my speaking abilities.

In my example, I would look at a crowd and think, "Are they judging me? What if they don't like what I have to say?" My mentor told me to have a different thought process. He said that every time I step on stage, I should think about the fact that I'm up there to share a story or help the crowd understand something, and that I am the expert of whatever subject is coming out of my mouth. I started stepping on stage with the mindset that I'm helping people, instead of wondering about their impression of me. That little tweak was what I needed, and I would've never seen it myself.

You never know where you can pick up another mentor. My mentors range from very outspoken people to some of the quietest, most soft-spoken people I know. You can only teach if you are taught, so if you think you know everything, you need to realize one thing: *you don't*. Find a few mentors who are just like you, and find a few mentors who are the complete opposite. Here's the awkward part—you may not always get along! But how much I learn from those meetings is far greater than what I learn from personalities that match mine.

Think about it this way: If you look at a sports car and see a sexy, sleek vehicle, chances are that people like you are going to see it the same way. Someone who's the opposite of you will tell you that it's not a nice car, and that you should take a look at the old, American muscle car. You might completely disagree (in this scenario, I'm with the American muscle), but you would have never thought to look at the muscle car if you weren't told to. You would've never thought to look elsewhere because all you ever saw was the beauty of a sports car, but you've neglected the beauty of an American muscle car. You never thought to look at it from a different perspective.

Let's look at it from another perspective. Think of a dream job that you're going for. You may have already made up your mind that it's the job for you because of all the perks, benefits, and responsibility. Your opposite might tell you that you're not ready, that you should look at a different job, or stick with the job that you're in for another year to properly gain the skills needed to perform at your dream job. You may hate hearing that, and you may resent the advice and even the person, but you should respect their point of view. You saw things one way, and your vision was blurred.

It's a good lesson to step back, look at the scenario from their lens, and take notes. I'm not saying you can't go after that dream job; I'm saying to take a look from their perspective and make sure you're hitting all four corners instead of just the two that you see.

NOTES

"I have always believed that when you have a voice, you have an obligation to use that voice to empower others."
—DIANE VON FURSTENBERG

CHAPTER 11

FEAR OF THE UNKNOWN

"Fear is not real. It is the product of thoughts you create . . .
Danger is very real, but fear is a choice."
—**CYPHER RAIGE,** *AFTER EARTH*

THE CAMBRIDGE DICTIONARY defines fear as "an unpleasant emotion or thought that you have when you are frightened or worried by something dangerous, painful, or bad that is happening or might happen." Here's my definition of fear: "An anxious feeling caused by what might happen, even though it's unknown."

What word sticks out to you the most?

Write it here: _____

The word that sticks out to me the most is *might*. I used

to let *might* stop me from doing a majority of the things I wanted to do. Writing this book is a perfect example—I was scared of what might happen if I didn't finish the book or have good content. The fear of the unknown can be such a rush in a positive way, but it truly is a double-edged sword. Let's dig in to some of my fears, what they used to be, and how I've managed to cut them loose.

For as long as I can remember, my list of fears was never-ending. I was always nervous about what people might think, what might happen, or what might not happen! If I peel the onion back, this anxiety most likely stemmed from my fear of judgement. Everyone's a bit scared of what people might think, right? At least that's what I thought, until I decided to drop that fear like bucket down a well.

Being judged is something that will happen *no matter what*. It was explained to me like this, and it really stuck with me: Prepare for judgement, because no matter what happens in life, you will be judged. When you go left, you get judged. When you go right, you get judged. When you go backwards in life, you get judged. When you find some sort of success and go forward, you get judged. If you stay in the same damn spot, you get judged. Do you see the common denominator there? Again, no matter what you do and where you go, you will always be judged. So, prepare for it; brush it like "dirt off your shoulder" (thanks Jay-Z), and move on with life.

Hearing that, I felt like a thousand pounds were lifted from my shoulders. I used to sit quietly, afraid to speak my mind or raise my hand when I had a chance to share, all because I feared being judged. Ladies and gentlemen, let me tell you this... I said, "bye bye bye" to that fear like NSYNC, and it has never returned to me. Amazing what can happen when you change your state of mind, am I right?

Okay, back to some of my fears. If I said I'm not afraid of anything now, I'd be lying. I still have some fears, but they mostly relate to my family... and sharks. Australia has changed the way I think about sharks because they are *everywhere.*

Growing up, I always feared my parents passing away. I would sit and cry at the slightest thought of something happening to my parents or sisters, or even my extended family... until it happened. When my dad passed away, that fear vanished like fairy dust. I realized that these things happen. I thought about it like this—if it were the other way around, and I passed away before my parents, the devastation would be at the maximum. But what happened was supposed to happen; it's the way life works.

My first experience with the death of a parent has given me strength to prepare for the second time around. Am I waiting for it to happen? Of course not. But one day, my mom will pass away, and that is just life. This may sound a bit harsh, but when I lost my dad, I knew that if I kept waiting for death to strike my family again, I would be living life in the shadows. Instead, I chose to cherish every single day with my family and work on the relationships that I have. That way, when the time comes to see the light, either my time or theirs, we can appreciate not only the time we spent together, but the relationship that we developed during the journey.

For those of you who know me personally (and I hope you know quite a bit about me by now, even if we haven't met), know that I take my health very seriously. I try to stay lean, fit, and healthy by working out, eating right, and shocking my body. Although I'm not a Dwayne Johnson or Vin Diesel (yet . . .), I have personal health goals that I intend to hit.

My motivation used to be fear-based until quite recently. I managed to stay fit after losing weight because I feared going back to the way things were—not only to the size that I was, but to the mindset that I was in. As I said earlier, my mindset was all wrong. I had zero motivation, I lacked the necessary confidence to get me anywhere, and I was very angry all the time. The fear of going back to the old Shiv kept me at the gym. At one point, I would even drop plans I made with a girlfriend to work out. When we first started dating, I couldn't commit to a second date because I hadn't scheduled my gym sessions that week (come on, Shiv!).

I've dropped that fear. I'm now extremely proud of what I've done, and I tell myself to never forget where I was and how far I've come. Sometimes dropping a fear is the easiest thing; you just need to give yourself *permission* to do it.

The only real fear we're born with is the fear of falling. Everything else is taught. Remember when you were a child and you were a daredevil? How did you grow up to be scared of the same things you did as a child? We are taught how to fear. Not just by society, but by our surroundings, schoolmates, family members, and acquaintances. As a child, I was terrified of bugs. Every time I saw one, I would do one of two things—kill it before it even moved, or scream and run away. Usually, it was scream and run away. But why was that the case?

My dad was always at work during the day. I was home with my mom and two sisters, who were scared of insects. Their reaction to spiders or flies was to scream and run away. I learned that fear of insects. My only response was to run away because I thought it was the right thing to do. I think at about seven or eight years old, I quickly dashway'd (new word, I made it up) to that fear because what my mom and sisters were doing was probably also taught to them. Maybe I didn't realize that at eight years old, but the fear was gone. Now, living in Australia, even spiders as big as my hand (no, I'm not exaggerating) don't really phase me.

There are a few more fears I could talk about, but here's what I want you to do. Write your fears down on a separate piece of paper—don't use the notes section. Write down your fears, write what makes you angry or even sad, and read it over about ten times. When you're done, I want you to rip it into pieces. You will feel much better than you did before you wrote all of that down. When I wrote my fears on a board at a conference, and broke through the board shortly after, I felt one hundred times better. If you think I'm exaggerating, it's probably because you haven't done the exercise!

Every single fear I wrote on that board is gone, and they

disappeared after I broke it. I have this board mounted on my wall in two pieces. I look at it every day and I smile. I smile because I think, "How the hell did these fears stop me from doing what I'm doing?" Well, not anymore, ladies and gents. It was a refresh button that I needed to hit, and damn, it felt good. Do the exercise and let me know how you feel afterward.

I wanted to bring up an experience in my first week here in Sydney. Whilst walking on the street, I was pushed and called a "terrorist." Out of the blue, a man literally walked up to me, put his hands on me, and uttered an extremely uneducated comment. It took all my might to not fight back, but I smiled, and simply told him that he's ignorant and should probably get his facts straight before he accuses anyone of such a thing (I definitely wasn't quite so calm).

People like that still exist in this world—people who are so stuck in their preconceptions that they only listen to what they see on TV or hear on the news, and decide to treat people unfairly because of propaganda. After I uttered my mouthful to the man, I started to walk away, but was hit in the back of the head. After I turned around, and after a little scuffle, we were broken apart by a few bystanders. I was ashamed of myself for even reacting, but I was so enraged, and even a tad afraid.

It was my first weekend in a brand-new country, where I didn't know anyone, and had no support and no idea what to do if it escalated. But I knew I had to say something, because if we stay quiet, no one will ever learn, and nothing will ever change. After we both walked away, a few bikers walked up to me (at this point, being scared was an understatement), and they told me they witnessed the entire thing. One of the older gentlemen looked at me and said, "We're all not like that." That, right there, restored my faith. The fact that someone actually walked up and apologized when they didn't have to was very special to me.

The moral of the story is this: A lot of us have experienced racial incidents. I'm a firm believer in staying quiet when your safety or your loved one's safety is in jeopardy. But I also believe that you should stand up for yourself when you get the chance. A lot of times, we experience these racial behaviors but nothing is ever said and done. The more people learn, the more educated they will become, and the less hatred there will be in this world. Don't be a pushover, be an educator.

NOTES

"Fear kills more dreams than failure ever will."
—UNKNOWN

CHAPTER 12

OPTIMIZING YOUR WEALTH

"Don't educate your children to be rich. Educate them to be happy, so they know the value of things, not the price."
—UNKNOWN

WEALTH CAN BE defined as a number of things—an abundance of valuable possessions, or a plentiful supply of a particular thing, like money, cars, houses, products, or anything tangible. What else can being wealthy mean? Take a look at the diagram below.

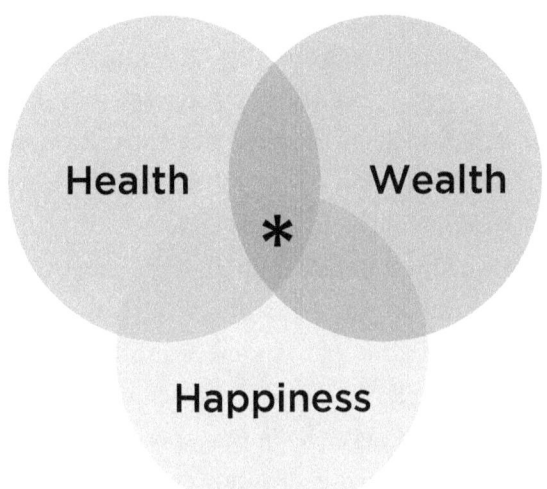

There are two here that I consider to be the most important definitions of wealth. You've probably heard people say, "Without your health, you are nothing." Well, guess what? Without your health, you *really are* nothing. What's the point of having all the possessions and riches in the world if you don't possess the health to actually enjoy those things? It baffles me that some individuals ignore their health just to make an extra buck. Some people never go to the gym, do not eat well, and don't do any sort of physical activity, just to make some cash. What's the point of that? Not having a healthy body and mind to enjoy your hard-earned money is not ideal, and I'm sure everyone can agree with that. If your health is in your control, then it's important that you handle it!

I couldn't imagine doing all the things I do if I didn't have a healthy body to keep up. If I realize that I'm physically lacking, I work hard to ensure that I keep up the next time. Why? Because I'm trying to achieve success with an optimal body and mind, so I can actually enjoy what's to come.

What's the one thing you will do to from now on to achieve a healthy body and mind?

The second most important part of the above diagram is being happy. This is probably right in line with your health. Do you know anyone that has more money than he can spend but is completely miserable? I definitely do, and I've promised myself to never be in that spot. Many people are unhappy despite "having it all"—however an individual may define that. True wealth, in my opinion, comes to those who are genuinely happy. We all have our ups and downs, but we never want to fall to our lowest low. To enjoy the wealth that we've achieved, we need to do whatever it takes to stay happy.

Which brings me to this question: Do you think wealth is a mindset? Can you be wealthy without having all the riches you want?

I like to think of wealth as a mental shift. I strongly believe you can attain wealth without the riches, the fancy cars, or the big houses. I always think of a time where I felt the at the peak of my happiness. That feeling is worth more than any amount of money. It's the feeling I get when I've genuinely helped someone; it's priceless to me.

I met a homeless man on the street in Sydney. I sat on a bench talking to him for about thirty minutes. This man, who possessed only the clothing on his back and a few cashews in his pocket, seemed like the happiest man I'd ever met. I actually approached him for the sole purpose of asking him if he was happy, and I got exactly what I was looking for. I asked him a number of questions about his life, like what happened, and why he was homeless.

The most important thing I got out of that conversation, and the part that will stay with me forever, was his take on happiness. He said, "You don't need a roof to be happy—you need the will." I was taken aback. I remember thinking that he was lying; there was no way he could be that happy. We chatted about his family, where they were, and his contact with them. He was very willing to converse, despite not knowing me. There I was, walking around with a few things that I thought I needed—fresh, new clothing, my phone, wallet, keys, and some cash—and there he was with virtually nothing, yet he was happier than me. At that moment, I realized what being wealthy really meant to me.

What does unlimited wealth mean to you, and how can you achieve it? This is a tough question for anyone to answer. But think about what it really means to have unlimited wealth. As I stated earlier, I think that the two most important ingredients for wealth are happiness and health. How can you optimize both ingredients to work for you, rather than you working for them?

Since staying healthy is a huge part of my routine, whether it's a morning workout or a few push-ups after work, I strive to do something active every day. My thought is that five minutes of physical activity is better than zero! So that's the health part. What about the happiness part? My surroundings play a *huge* part in keeping me happy. The people I surround myself with define who I am, and if they are like-minded, positive people, they keep me in check. Again, we all have our ups and downs. Life throws you challenges. It's how you react to those challenges that define you—how you overcome the hard times. I choose to keep happy, positive, and level-headed people around me, which keeps me happy. If I am feeling down, a simple call or text can put me right where I need to be. To be successful at managing your wealth, you need to fix your mindset. True wealth, for Shiv, means that he is happy, and he makes others around him happy. Like I said before, a smile is worth a thousand stories, but a real smile feels like it's worth a million bucks.

NOTES

"Wealth is the product of man's capacity to think."
—ALEXANDER POPE

What are your thoughts on wealth?

CHAPTER 13

TURNING A NEGATIVE INTO A POSITIVE— THE FULL CIRCLE

"Choosing to be positive and having a grateful attitude is going to determine how you're going to live your life."
—JOEL OSTEEN

I'M OFTEN ASKED, "What was the best day of your life?" When I think about it, there are so many great memories I've had, but I always go back to that day my father died—it was an honor spending his last hours with him.

On the other end of the spectrum is the day we found out that my dad had a brain tumor. As I mentioned in

Chapter 4, we grow up thinking our parents are superheroes with superhuman strength. I remember that my dad started to act a bit differently. He was weaker, he would fall, and he was losing weight rapidly. My reaction was anger, because I'd never seen my dad like that. I remember telling him to "get up" because he was "strong." I was such a naive kid.

This time for my family was a tough one; it was the first time that any of us had a major medical issue. We found out about the brain tumor on a Monday, and on Friday, it was removed successfully. Over the next few months and years, our family grew closer than ever. The best part was that my parents had more time together. My dad was a workaholic, who never took a sick day, and never took a vacation. He was always working. He was always stressed. After the brain tumor was removed, he pulled a 180-degree turn. He seemed stress free; he didn't go back to work, and he had time for his hobbies and for his family.

If you ask my mom today, she will tell you how much she cherishes those last four years she had with my dad. The tumor was a blessing in disguise because it gave my family, especially my mom, extra time.

Sometimes, events seem negative, but when we look back, they were all a big learning experience. We've all heard the saying "You win or you learn," and that's something that I live by. Whether it's the loss of a job, a failed subject at school, getting sick, or even getting into an argument with friends or family, try to learn from that experience. Tell yourself that things will be okay, because guess what? Things *will* be okay.

Gone are the days where we stay in the slump forever. Our intentions should always be to see something positive in every experience. Take this for example: If you get into an argument with a friend, maybe that argument was for a good reason. You and that friend stop communicating for a while—you stop talking, you stop texting, maybe pull the delete on "the Gram"—but you're still breathing, aren't you? Maybe you let someone negative out of your life.

What if you lose your job? I agree that this could be devastating, but how exciting is searching for the next big experience? You are about to step into a new world, with a new job and new tasks. That's something to be excited about! You not only get to learn new skills, you get to meet new people and create an entirely different network. Sometimes, the bad is actually the good—you just need to shine the light on the positive side of the experience.

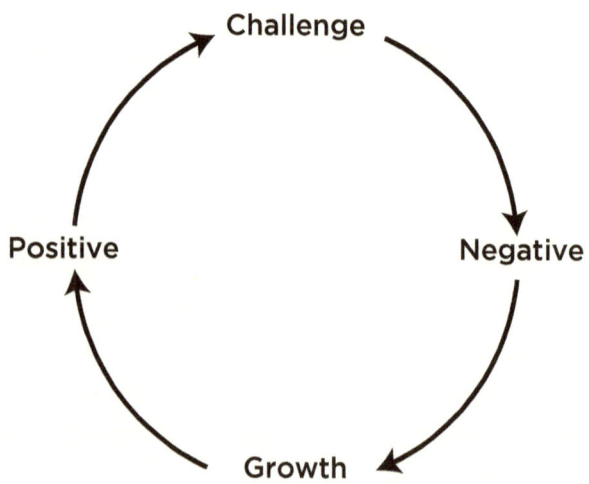

The above diagram shows exactly what I've experienced during the toughest events in my life. When I graduated university, I started work at a tech company in Canada, and I thought I was on top of the world. Four months later, I ended up getting laid off—so a kid straight out of university finds his dream job only to be told that his team has been made redundant. Great, right?

It was probably one of the best things to happen to me. The job was a positive experience, which posed a challenge, which led to negative thoughts, which taught me how the grown-up world really works. When I look back, the experience definitely goes back into the positive bucket. If I hadn't lost my job, I wouldn't have found the one I have now. My former job wouldn't have opened my eyes to a different road; I would've stagnated. Experiences are only tough if we make them tough. We can recover after almost anything, and learn from anything, so why not be a student all the time?

When I look at the diagram above, I can't help but bring up my dad again. His passing obviously struck our family with sadness and grief, but it also taught me gratitude, it taught me real strength, and it taught me how to be the man of the house. Gratitude is a topic I speak about often because I didn't appreciate it until my dad passed away. We always take things for granted, including our parents' presence in our lives. Gratitude is something I wish I learned before he passed, but the world works in mysterious ways. The entire experience I went through with my dad really taught me how to grow up. I started to look at death in a different way, and I realized that death isn't a bad thing. It's a natural thing. Death happens to all of us, so instead of fearing it, accept it. That was my example of turning a negative into a positive. What's yours?

NOTES

"A happy person is not a person who's always in a good situation, but rather a person who always has a good attitude in every situation."
—MARC CHERNOFF

CHAPTER 14

BREAK FREE

> "In order to save myself, I must destroy first
> the me I was told to be."
> **—THE DREAMER**

I'VE COME TO realize the few major points that really matter. Sometimes, we tell ourselves that the grass isn't always greener on the other side, but then we stop ourselves from even jumping over the fence to take a look. I wrote this book for you, the reader, to realize the importance of stepping out of your comfort zone; for you to realize your potential; for you to try something new, and keep pushing yourself to have the *I'll-give-it-a-shot* attitude. Constantly asking yourself "What's the worse than can happen?" is healthy, in my opinion. Yes, sometimes you get shot down, pushed around, and a little bit discouraged. But what happens next? You learn from the experience you just went through, and move on to becoming a better you. Breaking out of your comfort zone is about breaking the *regular effect*, and here's how you do it.

Step One: Put a magnifying glass over your social circle. We reviewed this in Chapter 9. If you are not hanging around with people who push you in the right direction, if your close friends do not support you following your dreams, cut them loose and find some new friends. Harsh? Yes. Essential? Absolutely. Your surroundings define you, which is why you need to take a deep look into your circle. Again, I'm not saying to never speak to them again, but create a bit of distance so that you can see them more clearly.

How often do you see a group of very successful people hanging out with someone who is the complete opposite? Maybe that person is extremely negative, and it's the attitude that separates them. What I'm saying is that if you surround yourself with people that have the right attitude and seem to be on an amazing trajectory, the chances are that you will be too. That's just the way the universe works!

Step Two: Never be afraid to put yourself out there. These days, many people commend me on putting myself out there and ask how I did it. Nike sums it up in just three simple words: "Just do it." Brilliant, if you ask me! A few years ago, I was not the Shiv that you're reading about today. Shiv a few years ago was timid, shy, and shackled to the restraints of the *regular effect*. Today, Shiv is confident, calm and collected, and always trying to challenge himself.

Rome wasn't build overnight. These things take time, but the initial step outside your comfort zone, the first crack of the *regular effect*, feels so good that you'll want to venture farther and farther. Imagine living under society's spell for twenty-five years, and you finally take that first step out of the safe zone. How good will that feel? It's like your first vacation outside of your home country. It feels good because everything is new. And what now? You can't wait until your next vacation, it's all you think about, and it motivates you. That's what breaking out of the *regular effect* feels like. It feels damn good, so I suggest you try it. You have to start somewhere. The universe works in strange ways. I find that if you actually put yourself out there, and make it known that you want to follow your dreams, eventually, that is exactly what will happen.

Step Three: Don't follow the money, follow what makes you happy. Sounds a bit mushy, right? Don't worry, I used to think so as well! In the past year or so, I've stopped following the money. Maybe my move to Australia played a big part. The move broke the *regular effect* into pieces. I moved with no friends, no family, no place to live, and managed to figure it out. That's not following the money—that's following the rush for a rich experience. "Following the money" means basing your entire life around making cash. Now, we all want to be financially free, and free in all the ways we deserve, but I disagree with living a life only to feed your bank account. To me, experiences are what make me rich, and the experiences that I've endured over the past few years make me feel like the richest man in the world. If you constantly follow the money, you get stuck in the *regular effect* trap. Society teaches us that to be successful, our bank accounts have to have six zeroes at the end of a number. At least, that's what I was taught. That was what success was defined as—the amount of money in your bank account.

As I got older, I started to realize that everyone has their own definition of success, and what success meant to me was having the ability to encounter multiple experiences through my travels, upward mobility and movement in my career, and of course, the most important point for me, to help as many people as I can in the process.

What does success mean to you? Write a few sentences below:

_____
_____
_____
_____
_____
_____
_____
_____

The drive to become a better *you* needs to be uncovered before breaking out of the *regular effect*. Finding that drive can be tough, but it's crucial in order to change your routine from the everyday to something new and refreshing.

How I found my drive was a little different, but I'd be happy for you to take it and make it your own force! I started forcing myself to speak. Sounds easy, but this was extremely tough for me. Just imagine a very overweight guy, shy, timid, scared of the world, who no one takes seriously. I had to force myself to not just speak to people, but present in front of multiple people. I took every opportunity, whether it was in front of my class for a project, or joining toastmasters (which I *highly* recommend), or even speaking with someone who you've never said a word to. This drove me to become a better Shiv. It gave me confidence, and made me realize some of the other changes I needed to make, like my weight. After building up my confidence for a while, I started to work out, see some progress, and realize that I could do literally anything that I wanted.

Today, I still have those driving factors. People always get nervous and fearful. Here's the difference. There are people that have so much fear that they won't go through with the next step, and there are people that have so much fear, but they say "*F* it" and go through with it anyway. I constantly choose the second option, and I highly recommend you do too #FindYourDrive.

I wrote this book with the sole purpose of helping individuals step out of their comfort zone and recognize the constraints that the *regular effect* has on all of us. As I stated in the preface, I never intended for this book to be read once and put back on the shelf. This book is for *you*, the reader, to refer back to constantly, to ensure that the goals you've been writing in the notes sections are achieved.

My hope is that this book will hold you accountable. Think of it as *me* holding you accountable! I encourage you to refer to the notes section at least once a month to ensure that you're taking the necessary steps to achieve—and even surpass—your goals. Don't forget to constantly set new goals. Hitting a goal is not the end, it's just the beginning. Set your next goal once you're close to achieving your initial one. For example, if your goal is to make $5 million in the next two years, why not make it $10 million in a year and a half? Make sure to make your goals *real*. Being rich isn't a goal, but $400,000 in one year is a goal.

If I can leave you with a few words, it would be this: Think of yourself five years from now. Where are you? What are you doing? Who are you with? Are you still in the same spot, or have you accomplished some of the goals you wrote in this book? If I said that you have 1,825 days to change, the chances are that you will use every minute of them wisely. Constantly think of the "future you." Think of your spouse, your car, your house, your happiness, your family. Think of where you'd like to be, and make it happen. Strive to hit that five-year goal—put it out to the universe and it will come to you, if you work hard enough for it.

Everything we do comes down to execution. If you choose not to execute the next steps to achieve your goal, nothing will happen. Don't be the same you in five years. Strive to be the best version of yourself, and strive to help those around you.

The *regular effect* is just an effect.

Break free.

ACCOUNTABILITY NOTES

"No one is coming to save you.
This life is 100% your responsibility. Plan accordingly."
—UNKNOWN

_____
_____
_____
_____
_____
_____
_____
_____
_____
_____
_____
_____
_____
_____
_____
_____
_____

www.ingramcontent.com/pod-product-compliance
Lightning Source LLC
Chambersburg PA
CBHW060534080526
44586CB00012B/726